HOLY CAPITALISM

HOLY CAPITALISM

Origins, Workings and Energy Catalyst

Dr. Richard E. Itteilag

authorHOUSE®

AuthorHouse™
1663 Liberty Drive
Bloomington, IN 47403
www.authorhouse.com
Phone: 1-800-839-8640

Published by AuthorHouse   07/11/2012

ISBN: 978-1-4772-1738-2 (sc)
ISBN: 978-1-4772-1737-5 (e)

Library of Congress Control Number: 2012910353

CONTENTS

PREFACE

In a recent book, "Civilization: The West and the Rest" by Niall Ferguson, he maintains that, beginning in the fifteenth century, the West, i.e., Western Europe, developed six powerful new concepts that the Rest of the world, primarily the East, did not have. In fact, the Far East, i.e., China, was considerably more advanced than the West prior to the fifteenth century. For example, in the thirteenth century, when Marco Polo visited the Orient as the first westerner, he was amazed by the volume of vessel traffic on the Yellow River, in both directions. Moreover, the Forbidden City, constructed by over a million workers in the heart of Beijing, using materials from all over China, had over a thousand buildings and was the greatest city in the known world. In addition, the Industrial Revolution was prefigured in China. The first blast furnace for smelting iron ore was not built in England in 1709, but in China before 200 B. C. The oldest iron suspension bridge in the world is not British, but Chinese.

This then begs the question: Why did the East, or more globally according to Ferguson called the Rest, stagnate?

There appear to be six main reasons missing in the development I y of the Rest:

1) competition,
2) science,
3) the rule of law,
4) modern medicine,
5) consumerism and
6) the work ethic.

These applications kept the West ahead of the Rest through:

1) charting global trade routes,
2) mastering scientific research,
3) instituting democratic governments,
4) doubling life expectancies,
5) developing the Industrial Revolution and
6) dramatically increasing human productivity.

At the time, essentially about a dozen Western countries, i.e., Austria, Belgium, France, Germany, Italy, the Netherlands, Portugal, Spain, Russia, the United Kingdom and the United States, controlled 60% of mankind's lifestyle and 80% of mankind's wealth. Of foremost importance, in effect, was global trade. Adam Smith, the famous English economist, noted that: "China seems to have been long stationary, and had probably long ago acquired that full complement of riches which is consistent with the nature of its laws and institutions. But this complement may be much inferior to what, with other laws and institutions, the nature of its soil, climate, and situation might admit of. A country which neglects or despises foreign commerce, and which admits the vessels of foreign nations into one or two of its ports only cannot transact the same quantity of business which it might do with different laws and institutions . . . By a more extensive navigation, the Chinese would naturally learn the art of using and constructing themselves all the different machines made use of in other countries, as well as the other improvements of art and industry which are practiced in all the different parts of the world."

Ultimately, the West outpaced the East over 500 years ago. However, the East has more than caught up currently with the West, and in some ways, I.e., through lower labor costs, computer technology, information technology (IT), etc., has actually surpassed the West, particularly in competitive trade. Retraining workers, computer automation of machinery, improved productivity and better cooperation between western governments and the business community can overcome this competitive trade disadvantage in the future.

From Ancient Philosophy (Plato) to Modern Economics (Joseph Schumpeter)

CHAPTER I

The Capitalist State as
The Welfare State

"The Gates/Ellison Unemployment Trap," or inverted innovations curve, shows that unemployment is sticky at high 9+% rates regardless of government policy, i.e., productivity rates from year 2000 at an index rate of 85% to year 2011 at an index rate of 115% v. unemployment rates from year 2000 of just under 6% to year 2011 at just over 9%. By observation, as productivity rises over time, unemployment rises in tandem showing a high correlation between the capitalist efforts to increase productivity to improve profits and the corresponding increases in unemployment to cut labor costs. Therefore, unemployment is sticky at 9+% rates. (2 graphs: productivity & unemployment here)

Most important, unemployment is 'structural,' i.e., skill-set gaps and limited work opportunities are actually endemic to modern-day capitalism, ergo a hidden and permanent characteristic of a capitalist economy.

Similarly, the share of working-age Americans who are in the labor force continues to decline to 63.6% in April, 2012, the lowest rate since December, 1981. Essentially, the rate has been declining since 2000, again while productivity has been increasing, as seen earlier.

In addition, the domino effect kicks-in and causes tepid growth rates in post-recession recoveries. The average growth rate in economic activity in the U.S. during periods of recovery from recessions has been 3.4% while the current recovery is barely growing at 2%. This weak economic growth has occurred while corporate profits, the stock market and productivity has grown. This is counterintuitive at best.

Moreover, digital technology, computerized machinery and a globalized workforce have brought down production costs. To counteract this, the Federal Reserve Bank monetized assets and pushed down interest rates. The result is falling prices and deflation. However, this also leads to speculative lending and borrowing. This artificially induced financial engineering serves to lift the prices of a favored class of assets, i.e., houses. And when the bubble bursts, I.e., the financial crisis of 2007-2008, credit contracts, leveraged businesses falter, inventories are liquidated and prices fall further.

A process of real deflation which, in turn, sets forth a new round of monetary intervention. In fact, a Wall Street Journal analysis of corporate financial reports found that cumulative sales, profits and employment in 2011 among members of the Standard & Poor's 500 stock index exceeded the totals of 2007, before the great recession and financial crisis. In 2007,companies generated an average of $378,000 in revenue per employee, while in 2011 that ratio rose significantly to $420,000. Their cash-flow and debt burden improved, as well.

The clear winners in the global economy are the BRIC (Brazil, Russia, India and China) countries with GDP annual growth rates in excess of 4% led by communist China.

To exacerbate the situation, the existence of "too big to fail" (TBTF) in corporate America is acute. It is the result of business consolidation to be positioned to compete in the global economy. For example. The five biggest U.S. banks control 52% of the country's financial assets. Hence, the moniker, TBTF, undermining the rules of market capitalism. Highly concentrated and complex banks are hard to manage by banking executives and even more difficult to regulate by government watchdogs. The recent $2 billion investment loss by JPMorgan Chase is a case in point. TBTF then becomes in a financial crisis like 2008 a taxpayer bailout putting increased downward pressure on a recessionary economy and accelerating calls in Congress for increased and more potent financial controls Instead of limiting financial choice through heavy economic concentration, the U. S. economy, therefore capitalism, TBTF banks should divest or sell-off assets thereby becoming smaller and less complex to manage and regulate.

Communist philosopher, Karl Marx, postulated that capitalism will destroy itself. In fact, Austrian economist, Joseph Schumpeter, in his ground-breaking work, "Capitalism, Socialism and Democracy," finds that Marx is correct: capitalism suffers from 'creative destruction' or creating/destroying itself continuously.

Both economists pointed to failures in the capitalist system. In fact, it is not the failures of capitalism, I.e., inflation, unemployment, deficits, trade imbalances, etc., but the successes, in particular, i.e., increased productivity, rising profits, trade surpluses, etc., that present itself in high, 'sticky' unemployment. Business investment in computer software, i.e., the Information Technology (IT) sector, guarantees less workers are hired and, more important, more workers are laid off, thereby raising unemployment.

Thus, capitalism's growth hinges on the demand side of the economy where lower taxes are more stimulative, not the supply side, such as infrastructure or government spending on repairing bridges and paving roads, which are only moderately stimulative, temporary and finite. Witness the recent Obama stimulus package that was ineffective at overcoming the Great Recession and only protected the economy from a deep and prolonged depression. In fact, unemployment remained 'sticky' near 9%.

To effect the demand side of the economy, therefore, tax policy reform is critical or the policy implementation of the Austrian School of economic theory: repatriating corporate overseas profits, capital gains tax reductions, payroll tax holidays and lower W2 wage withholdings. These policy actions, for example, would stimulate the demand-side of a capitalist economy where all economists agree the problem lies.

The experiences in capitalist Sweden and Iceland, specifically since the financial crisis of the mid-2000s, suggest demand-side policies work. Both countries devalued their currencies, cut taxes, balanced federal budgets and liberalized foreign trade.

The U.S. version of capitalism currently emphasizes the service sector of the economy such as real estate and retailing, not the manufacturing sector, like steel and auto production.

The long-term decline in manufacturing has eroded a major source of stable jobs that pay well and that are more reflective of the U.S. workforce. The construction boom of the mid-2000s helped offset those loses, until the housing market collapsed in the Great Recession of 2007 and took home builders with it.

And more important, the slow economic recovery since 2007 has put a premium on productivity, giving companies incentives to invest in new technology that lets them produce more with fewer workers, a trend that has spread from manufacturing into the service sector thereby only exacerbating the unemployment problem.

The challenge then, is not just putting more people back to work, but helping to train and rehabilitate the long-term unemployed, thereby reversing a multi-decade stagnation in the labor market, and finding a new source of jobs to rebuild the middle class. Long-term unemployment might be a bigger problem than high. 'sticky' unemployment.

A continued weak economic recovery since the recession ended more than two years ago, has stalled employment growth that is contingent on robust real economic activity.

And this situation is a 'catch 22' because high unemployment helps to put the brakes on economic growth and, in turn, stagnant economic activity accelerates unemployment. Some 5.6 million people have been unemployed for at least six months, while 3.9 million of them have been unemployed for a year or more. Research shows that the longer people are unemployed, the harder it is to find work. Many of the people out of work the longest likely will never work again!

When it comes to unemployment, 'holy capitalism' can be 'hellish.' U.S. workers are ill prepared for the 21st century labor market that requires information technology (IT) skill sets, I.e., computer software knowledge and software engineers, not machine-oriented skill sets and blue-collar laborers.

The private equity investment process, I.e., business formation and/or acquisition, is free market capitalism at its best. Private equity helps corporate performance and in the long run leads to higher employment and higher wages. The resultant improved economic activity raises tax revenues which in turn fosters 'the welfare state' through government spending or 'Robin Hood' capitalism, I.e., take from the rich to give to the poor.

In a January 30, 2011 Op Ed article in the Wall Street Journal entitled: "The Coming Tech-led Boom," Mr. Mark P. Mills, a physicist and founder of the Digital Power Group, and Mr. Julio M. Ottino, dean of the McCormick School of Engineering and Applied Sciences at Northwestern University, argue that the United States (U.S.) emerged from 19 recessions since 1912 with a century of phenomenal growth, where Americans experienced 700% growth in wealth today. They attribute much of that growth to the technological advances in electrification, telephony, the dawn of the automobile age, the inventions of stainless steel and the radio amplifier, which fostered this economic growth and prosperity.

They believe that, in January, 2012, we are at the cusp of three grand technological transformations and the potential to rival that of the past century:

1) big data,
2) smart manufacturing, and
3) wireless revolution.

Added to these technological advances, is the fact that the U. S. will have one of the youngest demographics in the world. They deduce that with youth comes energy, curiosity and innovation, vital to promote economic growth.

However, these factors only add to the economic morass that pervades the U.S. economy. More efficient manufacturing will only put more people out of work.

And, a younger population, will only add more inexperienced people to the unemployment rolls. Therefore, it is more likely that the U. S. unemployment rate will remain sticky at 9+%.

In a survey, conducted in October, 2011, of Harvard Business School graduates, in which nearly 10,000 respondents participated, the general concensus of the graduate business executives was that the United States (U.S.) competitiveness in the world would worsen over the next three years.

The result would cause U.S. prosperity to decline.

There were a number of structural changes, in addition to the weakened economy from the Great Recession of 2007, outlined by the respondents causing this competitive disadvantage. First, there are fundamental gaps in worker skills and opportunities in the U.S. compared to the rest of the world, and Second, while the U.S. faced a similar competitive disadvantage in the 1980s, the competitive advantage was achieved by essentially one country, i.e., Japan.

Today, however, the existing competitive edge is successfully exhibited by much of the entire world at large!

In the 1980s, government and business joined forces to implement policy changes that gave the U. S. business community the tools necessary to compete successfully. Currently, however, the debate in the U.S. Is so partisan and fragmented that the U.S. policymakers are not even focusing on the correct problem.

The fact is that the critical problem is not income inequality, which, in fact, is the result of the problem, but a gap in skill sets and work opportunities.

While the government sector will need to play an important role in solving this problem, the business community must step-up to the plate with concrete strategies and innovative ideas.

In an Op-Ed article in the Wall Street Journal on Wednesday, January 25, 2012, John B. Taylor, professor of economics at Stanford University, stated the economic difficulties of the late 1970s, that mirror the current morass of persistent high unemployment and lack of confidence in government leadership, did not change until Ronald Reagan became president in 1980. President Reagan believed in economic freedom, limited government and the teachings of economists like Friedrich von Hayek and Milton

Friedman. The Reagan appointees led by treasury secretary, George Shultz, submitted a memo to Reagan entitled: "Economic Strategy for the Reagan Administration" which called for a complete change in economic policy from the Carter Administration with a long-term point of view to allow for the time, coherence and the predictability necessary for success. That long-term predictability lasted past the Reagan Administration but has waned with the Obama Administration, thus exacerbating the U.S. economic slowdown and international trade competitive disadvantage for America.

Source: Bureau of Labor Statistics, Productivity and Cost

Sector: Nonfarm Business
Measure: Labor Productivity (Output Per Hour)
Duration: index, 2005=100
Base Year: 2005

Year	Qtr1	Qtr2	Qtr3	Qtr4	Annual
1990	69.204	69.780	70.071	69.461	69.629
1991	69.627	70.667	71.099	71.427	70.703
1992	72.620	73.153	73.886	74.445	73.529
1993	73.903	73.583	73.870	74.388	73.937
1994	74.794	74.728	74.287	74.972	74.695
1995	74.720	74.836	74.939	75.505	75.001
1996	76.163	77.011	77.258	77.306	76.938
1997	77.033	77.935	78.588	78.895	78.116
1998	79.345	79.832	80.910	81.538	80.411
1999	82.325	82.396	83.077	84.505	83.080
2000	84.188	86.092	86.105	86.955	85.901
2001	86.670	88.234	88.777	90.033	88.413
2002	91.944	92.053	92.920	92.866	92.445
2003	93.710	94.983	97.165	97.532	95.848
2004	97.675	98.467	98.631	98.764	98.386
2005	99.779	99.574	100.342	100.303	100.000
2006	100.924	101.031	100.478	101.146	100.894
2007	101.085	101.943	103.151	103.648	102.456
2008	102.968	103.583	103.369	102.488	103.104
2009	102.822	104.904	106.536	107.928	105.523
2010	109.134	109.473	109.961	110.451	109.758
2011	110.170	110.080	110.564	110.891(R)	110.249
2012	110.752				

Source: Bureau of Labor Statistics, Current Population Survey

Source: Bureau of Labor Statistics, Current Population Survey

Seasonally Adjusted
Series title: Unemployment Rate
Labor force status: Unemployment rate
Type of data: Percent or rate
Age: 16 years and over

Unemployment Rate
Labor force status: Unemployment rate
Type of data: Percent or rate
Age: 16 years and over

Year	Jan	Feb	Mar	Apr	May	Jun	Jul	Aug	Sep	Oct	Nov	Dec
2002	5.7	5.7	5.7	5.9	5.8	5.8	5.8	5.7	5.7	5.7	5.9	6.0
2003	5.8	5.9	5.9	6.0	6.1	6.3	6.2	6.1	6.1	6.0	5.8	5.7
2004	5.7	5.6	5.8	5.6	5.6	5.6	5.5	5.4	5.4	5.5	5.4	5.4
2005	5.3	5.4	5.2	5.2	5.1	5.0	5.0	4.9	5.0	5.0	5.0	4.9
2006	4.7	4.8	4.7	4.7	4.6	4.6	4.7	4.7	4.5	4.4	4.5	4.4
2007	4.6	4.5	4.4	4.5	4.4	4.6	4.7	4.6	4.7	4.7	4.7	5.0
2008	5.0	4.9	5.1	5.0	5.4	5.6	5.8	6.1	6.1	6.5	6.8	7.3
2009	7.8	8.3	8.7	8.9	9.4	9.5	9.5	9.6	9.8	10.0	9.9	9.9
2010	9.7	9.8	9.8	9.9	9.6	9.4	9.5	9.6	9.5	9.5	9.8	9.4
2011	9.1	9.0	8.9	9.0	9.0	9.1	9.1	9.1	9.0	8.9	8.7	8.5
2012	8.3	8.3	8.2	8.								

CHAPTER II

Plato's Ideal State

Plato: I came, I saw, I philosophized!

Plato, like Socrates and Aristotle before him, shaped western thought and state government. In effect, he came, he saw and he philosophized. However, Plato's contribution far surpassed the metaphysical and, even, the practical or political. Plato, in fact, set the fundamentals for capitalism, the economic engine of the modern western world. Plato, in The Republic, advocated the rule of philosopher kings, without any institutional checks and balances. He proposed the 'Ideal State' but believed, however, that the ideal state was fatally flawed. This he believed was due to the fact that it could not cope with the key insight of liberal politics: absolute power corrupts absolutely.

The modern-day Austrian philosopher, Karl Popper, interpreted this ideal state as a totalitarian government, much like Nietzsche for Nazism or Hegel and Marx for Communism.

In fact, Plato believed that absolute power would corrupt politics. But Plato believed more deeply that: absolute power actually destroys not merely corrupts.

This destructive quality of capitalism hinges on the demand side of the economy through lower taxes not the supply side such as infrastructure or government spending on repairing bridges and paving roads To effect the demand side of the economy, tax policy reform is critical or the policy implementation of the Austrian School of economic theory. Ergo, repatriating corporate overseas profits, capital gains tax reductions, payroll tax holidays and lower W2 wage withholdings, for example, would stimulate the demand-side of a capitalist economy.

The U.S. version of capitalism currently emphasizes the service sector of the economy such as real estate and retailing, not the manufacturing sector like steel and auto production.

The long-term decline in manufacturing has eroded a major source of stable jobs that pay well. The construction boom of the mid-2000s helped offset those loses, until the housing market collapsed in the Great Recession of 2007 and took home builders with it. And the slow economic recovery since 2007 has put a premium on productivity, giving companies incentives to invest in new technology that lets them produce more with fewer workers, a trend that has spread from manufacturing into the service sector.

The challenge then, is not just putting people back to work, but helping to train and rehabilitate the long-term unemployed, reversing a multi-decade stagnation in the labor market, and finding a new source of jobs to rebuild the middle class.

Thus, long-term unemployment might be a bigger problem than high unemployment. A continued weak economic recovery since the recession ended more than two years ago, has stalled employment growth that is contingent on robust real economic activity.

And this situation is a 'catch 22' because high unemployment helps to put the brakes on economic growth and stagnant economic activity accelerates unemployment. The ideal state is better understood as the operative quality of capitalism: it constantly destroys itself then creates itself all over again.
For example, while capitalism can falter, i.e., destroy itself through high unemployment and recessions, it can regenerate itself, i.e., improve itself through recoveries and escalating employment.

In support of Plato, Nobel laureate in economics, Friedrich von Hayek, is often associated with his critique of socialist systems. He submits that there is in society a "knowledge problem." Simply, economic life requires the coordination of individual planning. The relevant knowledge for economic planning is dispersed rather than concentrated in society. This makes coordination a serious challenge in a capitalist system, and virtually impossible in a socialist system. A socialist central planner could never collect and process the necessary data to provide detailed guidance in any given circumstance that develops in society.

Plato resolved this apparent paradox by depicting the ideal state in The Republic as the political body that would be ruled by a new breed of leaders, I.e., the philosopher king, or in today's modern western world, the economist president or prime minister. A current case in point, for example, is recently elected economist and president, Mario Monti of Italy. President Monti is instituting supply-side economic principles to jump-start Italy's struggling, debt-ridden economy. He has raised the retirement age and is transforming labor markets by reducing barriers to entry in previously protected professions from pharmacy and baking to taxi driving. He has become widely respected by the electorate. More competition, he believes, means more jobs and a higher standard of living.

These philosopher kings or economists, not seeking power for their own purposes, but accepting the power to govern after democratic elections, administer checks and balances on politics and regulations. These rulers are capable of gaining knowledge of what is good, as opposed to the mere opinions and self-serving conventions that ordinary rulers value. By seeking this lofty, altruistic goal, Plato creates a new role for culture and a new environment for politics. It is from this complex transformative vision of society that the fundamental workings of modern western economics, I.e., capitalism, are born.

CHAPTER III

Origins of Capitalism

It is not until the Middle Ages that capitalism is perfected by the Knights Templar during the Crusades in Europe. The Crusaders in circa 1033 were escorted, I.e., protected in effect, by the Knights Templar enroute to Jerusalem to fight the Moslems. The Knights Templar were paid for their protection by charging rent, i.e., interest. The Templars were essentially bankers lending money to the Crusaders for their supplies on the long journey from western Europe to the Middle East. The Templars, therefore, it is believed, founded the Swiss banking system because Templars were the first bankers charging interest, I.e., called rent at the time, because the Catholic Church forbade lending money as usury. The Templars issued travelers checks, safe deposit boxes and lines of credit.

Scotland, through the powerful Sinclair family (Edward Sinclair, father), was the site of the last stronghold of the Templars. The Templars were driven from France in 1314 and relocated with the Sinclair family in Scotland at Roslind Castle.

The Templars were popular during the Crusades from 1000-1320s a.d. Western Europeans, at the time, believed as Christians that they collectively owned a tract of territory in the Middle East, i.e., the Holy Land, on which none of them ever lived but had an unquestionable right to it because their Saviour had died on it and it was their religious duty to recapture. In fact, the Holy Land had been in Moslem hands since the 7th century.

Since the Templars were great seafarers with a large shipping fleet; they traded extensively with the Holy Land; they transported Crusaders to the Holy Land during the Crusades and they often were hired as warriors to protect wealthy European families. Moreover, they were believed to have discovered Oak Island, New Fondland (Canada), and to be the first settlers in the New World, centuries before Columbus and the Spaniards.

Today, in the 21st century, in fact, for the first time in history, the majority of the world's 195 countries either have a capitalist economy or are trying to form a capitalist economy.

In 1950, about 40% of the global population was living under totalitarian communist rule, and an additional 25%-35% lived in countries with governments that were either openly socialist or tending to be socialist.

According to Schumpeter, capitalism, democracy and "ethical imperialism" are intertwined and must be dissected. In fact, Schumpeter believed that much of the western world was drifting towards socialism. The Great Depression of 1929 and the resultant staggeringly high unemployment of 17% that continued to 1939, indicated that capitalism wasn't working and that the communist structure of the Soviet Union, with no unemployment, was working and, therefore, superior. It appeared that socialist planning was working while the capitalist market economy was faltering.

Socialism also appealed to many as more egalitarian since it exhibited the absence of class distinctions and the fair distribution of wealth and income. In fact, Russia was the only country pursuing these goals effectively.

CHAPTER IV

Capitalism:
Democracy v. Communism

A. Capitalism

In 1950, about 40% of the global population was living under totalitarian-like communist rule. An additional 25-35% lived in countries with governments that were either openly socialist or tending to be socialist. 'Creative Destruction,' the phrase coined by Austrian economist, Joseph Schumpeter in 1942, is the capitalist process that endlessly replaces old products and services with new ones, which is 'the essential fact about capitalism.'

Constant, relentless change is the hallmark of capitalism and it is the spiritual challenge of its culture. The Holy Grail is not the Stock Exchange but the 'gamble of capitalism.' Any success or failure in culture often is witnessed in a business endeavor. Therefore, the principle problem with capitalism is how to harness its power and keep it from 'destroying itself.' Capitalism is both fragile and difficult to develop. More important, is that capitalism is near impossible to sustain.

Ceaseless innovation, and the resultant reduction in the workforce it causes, I.e., unemployment in the form of creative destruction, brings the heavy social costs of capitalism. Family fortunes are destroyed, whole communities are damaged and an intellectual class is alienated from the very materialism that brought it the leisure to conceptualize metaphysical ideas.

At its core, capitalism exhibits all the fundamental human truths people face in the real world. Are the material fruits of capitalism, the most productive economic system in the world, worth the social costs? Are greed, venality, despoliation of the environment and the wide disparities in wealth and income, acceptable prices to pay for capitalism? Can a robust capitalist system be successfully combined with an authoritarian regime, as China has attempted? Or are they mutually exclusive?

Should economic development precede democratic government, as in China, or follow in its wake, as in India? Can the mixed economies of Japan and western Europe, in which the hand of government guidance regulates the functioning of the market, continue to be successful as they have been since their birth in the 1940s? Today, Japan has experienced the 'lost decade' and the western European countries of Greece, Spain, Italy and Portugal, are struggling with massive debts, high levels of unemployment and persistent recessions! And what is the precise role of capitalism in the battles over worldwide modernization involving Islamic terrorism and the spreading Arab Spring, I.e., the uprisings in Egypt, Tunisia, Libya and Syria?

The actual and prospective performance of the capitalist system is such that it is bound to succeed and will not buckle under its own weight from economic failure. However, capitalism's very success undermines the social institutions which protect it, and inevitably creates conditions in which it will not be able to live and which strongly point to socialism as heir apparent. But this form of socialism is only a sub-set of capitalism, I.e., the welfare state. It presents itself in the tax system that encourages charitable giving by allowing generous deductions from ordinary income to avoid taxes. In addition, capitalism has a long history of philanthropy and the formation of charitable foundations such as the Bill and Melinda Gates Foundation, the Ford Foundation, etc. This phenomenon is known as: 'the idealism inherent in the reality of capitalism.' The moral basis for capitalism lies in the Protestant ethic, I.e. Christianity. Since the tenets of capitalism are transposed into religion and it, in turn, manifests an altruistic kind of democratic persuasion, there is no longer any need for logical scruples about the 'Common Good and Ultimate Values.' All this is settled for the capitalist by God's plan whose purpose defines and sanctions all transactions. That which seemed indefinite and imprecise, becomes definitive and highly accurate. The voice of the people, in essence, represents the voice of God. And business decisions are made on empirical analysis not social conscious.

A market system can not work properly if a society aims to dole out rewards and punishments like a professor in a lecture room. Market institutions are anonymous and blind. Imposing upon them any preordained scheme of merit and reward will just make coordination between individuals, I.e., wealth creation, more difficult. In fact, capitalism promotes income inequality. For example, according to an Op Ed article in the Wall Street Journal on April 24, 2012, Peter Diamond and Emmanuel Saez state that the share of pre-tax income accruing to the top 1% of earners in the U. S. has more than doubled to about 20% in 2010 from less than 10% in the 1970s. At the same time, the average federal income tax rate on top earners has declined significantly. This trend has increased the U. S. income concentration in the top 1% of earners to one of the highest levels in history. Increasing taxes on the rich to raise revenue can partially reduce capitalism's fiscal deficits.

While there is a risk of reducing economic growth, especially in a deep, current recession, history documents that in the post-war U. S. higher top tax rates tend to go with greater economic growth—not lower!. In fact, GDP annual growth per capita averaged 1.68% between 1980 and 2000 when top tax rates were relatively low, while growth averaged 2.23% between 1950 and 1980 when top tax rates were high, I.e., at or above 70%.

Capitalism and Monetary Policy

The growing disparity between the rich and the poor, I.e., the 1% v. the 99% or the 1% rule, is caused by the Federal Reserve Bank not runaway entrepreneurial capitalism. The relentless expansion of the money supply or credit by the Fed creates artificial disparities based on political privilege and economic power.

In an Op Ed article in the April 20, 2012 edition of The Wall Street Journal, Mark Spitznagel claims that the 18th-century philosopher, David Hume, pointed out that when money is inserted into the economy from a government printing press, i.e., the Fed, it is not distributed evenly but "confined to the coffers of a few persons, who immediately seek to employ it to advantage."

In the 20th century, Austrian School economist, Ludwig von Mises demonstrated how an increase in the money supply is beneficial to those who get it first and is detrimental to those who get it last. Monetary inflation is a process, not a static effect. It is a dynamic, pernicious process and creates imbalances and dislocations. The expansion of credit is uneven in the economy, which results automatically in wealth redistribution.

B. Socialism

Competitive leadership contains the fundamental facts of democracy. Therefore, the relationship between democracy and the socialist order lies in the interpretation of competition. Socialists claim that democracy implies socialism and that there can not be true democracy without socialism. Capitalists, however, submit that a planned economy, or socialist state, is completely incompatible with democracy.

In fact, the socialists and the capitalists are both right, and, for the same reasons. Through government welfare programs, the capitalist state artificially promotes democracy, while the socialist state enforces financial equality by imposing authoritarian rule and taking wealth from the rich and giving it to the poor.

Similar results through dramatically different means. While capitalism relies on free will to reach equality, socialism relies on the heavy hand of government to enforce equality. The end does not justify the means! Riots and unrest result causing chaos and, ultimately, revolution. Witness the American Revolution and the resultant French Revolution in the 18th century. Centralized governments allocate resources badly regardless of their intensions.

The very nature of centralization makes it impossible to collect and compute all the information that is needed. This is true for capitalism as it is for a government-led welfare state, I.e., the European "social model." Von Hayek pointed out that theories centered on the notion of "social justice" try to resemble, at the level of the "great society," the nature of smaller groups. In the smaller groups in which human brings lived for most of history, people were compensated and advanced in society due to some shared vision of merit and worthiness. This also happens within larger societies. There are organizations, like corporations, in which people are rewarded because they score well in a particular metric.

According to von Hayek, small, self-organized, voluntary aggregates of people should be free to pursue their idea of "merit" as they wish provided that they take full responsibility for their efforts. However, a big society, I.e., one based on cooperation with strangers on a large scale, such as a state, should not attempt to play the game of the "just" distribution because it is not designed to do it. The European social model that trade unions and political parties still defend with such passion was ill-conceived from the start. This European model has now reached its Malcolm Gladwell "tipping point," economic collapse and social unrest!

Social Justice v. Economic Liberty

Today, the debate is between the party of social justice and the party of economic liberty. This debate dates back potentially to Karl Marx's critique of commercial society. In fact, it is suggested to have originated in the 1970s.

It was in 1971 that John Rawls' "A Theory of Justice" appeared laying out the basis of social justice. Rawls argues that society's institutions should be arranged to benefit the least advantaged. His theory became the template for the left-leaning liberal sect in America. Just five years later, von Hayek published "The Mirage of Social Justice," a defense of free market capitalism. In it he denounced the whole notion of social justice, describing it as a "will-of-the-wisp"—a "quasi-religious superstition." Von Hayek said that social justice is a "mark of demagogy" as well as "empty and meaningless." Americans, therefore, have been forced to choose between social justice and economic freedom. On the one side is the condescending left liberalism and, on the other, the heartless libertarians, i.e., CNN (Occupy Wall Street) v. Fox (Tea Party). It is thought that there can not be any "common ground" between the two!

In a new book by John Tomasi of Brown University, "Free Market Fairness," he suggests a "market democracy," a hybrid mix of economic liberty and social justice. A break from the two prevailing conflicting views. This market democracy is a result of the recent economic transition in America from a post-industrial state to a global Internet economy. He theorizes that people of all income levels today value the right to make economic choices while supporting programs that adjust society for inequalities.

CHAPTER V

Holy Capitalism as the Welfare State, i.e., the "Common Ground"

Holy capitalism, as the welfare state, is the answer, or "common ground" between social justice and economic liberty. To support the theory that capitalism mirrors the welfare state or the "common ground," a number of factors are evident.

First, capitalism offers its workers unemployment insurance. Workers put out of work are subsidized for up to 11.5 weeks with funds while the unemployed seek work.

Second, food stamps are issued to these job seekers while out of work.

Third, charitable contributions are deducted from the taxable income of wage earners which become another source of funds available to job seekers in need.

Fourth, social security benefits are available for the elderly poor as well as social security disability funds for those unable to work due to health issues.

Thus, there is a sizable safety net, i.e., the welfare state, for the needy imbedded in capitalism. And, in fact, holy capitalism achieves the proverbial "common ground."

CHAPTER VI

Monetary Policy

In an Op Ed article in the April 20, 2012 edition of The Wall Street Journal, Mark Spitznagel claims that the 18th-century philosopher, David Hume, pointed out that when money is inserted into the economy from a government printing press, I.e., the Fed, it is not distributed evenly but "confined to the coffers of a few persons, who immediately seek to employ it to advantage."

In the 20th century, Austrian School economist, Ludwig von Mises, demonstrated how an increase in the money supply is beneficial to those who get it first and is detrimental to those who get it last. Monetary inflation is a process, not a static effect. It is a dynamic, pernicious process and leads to economicdislocations. The expansion of credit is uneven in the economy, which results automatically in wealth redistribution.

CHAPTER VII

Conclusion: The Idealism Inherent in the Reality of Capitalism

In the U.S., the capitalist government could be streamlined and focused strategically on overcoming the institutional barriers to employment like currently in Italy. In particular, the U.S. Department of Labor could be abolished and a new Department of Human Resources, I.e., Department of Employment, could be surgically removed from the U. S. Department of Health and Human Resources. This new, specialized government department would have a master, worldwide database of job listings, an internship program matching employers to qualified applicants and a robust training/certification program for 21st century job skills in fields like information technology (IT), energy efficiency site management (green/LEED buildings), etc.

Today's U.S. capitalist system hinges on the demand side of the economy through lower taxes not the supply side such as infrastructure or government spending on repairing bridges and paving roads

To effect the demand side of the economy, tax policy reform is critical or the policy framework of the Austrian School of economic theory where repatriating corporate overseas profits, capital gains tax reductions, payroll tax holidays and lower W2 wage withholdings, for example, would stimulate the demand-side of a capitalist economy. In fact, the Kennedy-Johnson tax cuts during the recession of the early 1960s pushed the unemployment rate below 5% and the GDP growth rate above 5% from 2%. Tax policy in a capitalist system, therefore, should be concerned with competition not fairness.

The U.S. version of capitalism currently emphasizes the service sector of the economy such as real estate and retailing, not the manufacturing sector like steel and auto production.

In fact, the long-term decline in manufacturing has eroded a major source of stable jobs that pay well. The construction boom of the mid-2000s in the U.S. helped offset those loses, until the housing market collapsed in the Great Recession of 2007 and took home builders with it. And the slow economic recovery since 2007 has put a premium on productivity, giving companies incentives to invest in new technology that lets them produce more with fewer workers, a trend that has spread from manufacturing into the service sector.

The challenge then for U.S. capitalism is not just putting people back to work, but helping to train and rehabilitate the long-term unemployed, reversing a multi-decade stagnation in the labor market, and finding a new source of jobs to rebuild the middle class.

Thus, long-term unemployment might be a bigger problem than high unemployment. A continued weak economic recovery since the recession ended more than two years ago, has stalled employment growth that is contingent on robust real economic activity.

And this situation is a 'catch 22' because high unemployment helps to put the brakes on economic growth and stagnant economic activity exacerbating unemployment.

CHAPTER VIII

Energy, the Robust Resource Base, as Catalyst

Issues in 21St. Century Energy Economics

A. Conservation Revisited

Energy efficiency is the 'fifth' energy resource and that, in fact, it is the 'Current' big thing. The United States (U.S.) has made great strides in energy efficiency, i.e., 50% reduction in energy use per unit of output since the 1970s, Europe has lagged far behind. In particular, the Europeans do not place a high priority on energy efficiency. Europe appears to be more concerned with climate change and implementing a 'cap and trade' program to regulate carbon dioxide (CO2) emissions. While a 'cap and trade' program might have the positive side effects of also reducing energy consumption, i.e., increased conservation, this highly restrictive policy would have the unintended consequences of reducing economic output and exacerbating unemployment when the European economy is at a severely fragile point.

Energy efficiency is like providing the economy a 'fifth' fuel besides natural gas, electricity, oil and coal. Energy efficiency continued to break new ground in the U.S., but at a decreasing pace. Energy efficiency appears to be the best path to improving economic activity, creating new jobs and mitigating climate change.

While it is catchy to say that energy conservation is the 'fifth' energy resource, that would be flat-out wrong! In fact, energy efficiency is the 'faux' energy resource. The United States has been promoting energy efficiency and conservation since the first oil shock in the early 1970s and is still the largest consumer of energy worldwide.

The implications for industry are straight forward. For example, energy conservation can only be effective if the conversion to high-efficiency equipment can pay back the investment in three years or less. Therefore, energy conservation will always compete with other business investments first. Essentially, industry must rely on fossil fuels like natural gas, oil and coal for the next 100 years at a minimum. However, industry must replace obsolete rquipment with new, high-efficiency equipment over the useful life of the equipment. This will ensure that the energy footprint for industry will contract over time, but at a very slow, deliberate pace. The only conservation and renewable fuel that the U.S. can rely on today is hydro power, but only for less than 5% of electric power generation.

For the immediate timeframe, industry will be faced with mandated efficiency standards in the form of 'demand response' programs. These required efficiency standards are prominent in the western U.S., primarily in California, but are rapidly being adopted nationwide. Ultimately, from an industry perspective, energy efficiency or conservation can reduce industry's input costs and achieve higher product margins while being good corporate citizens and silent environmentalists.

B. Energy Independence and Policy Act of 2007 (EPact of 2007)

Lighting Efficiency

1) appliance bulbs, "rough service" bulbs, colored bulbs, plant lights and 3-way bulbs, are exempt from 25% greater efficiency standards
2) 40 watt and more than 150 watt-plus bulbs are also exempt
3) stage and Malibu lighting are exempted, as well

Buildings Efficiency

1) creates Office of Commercial High Performance Green Buildings in the Department of Energy (DOE) to promote more efficient buildings
2) creates a nationwide zero-net energy initiative for commercial buildings built after 2025

Industrial Efficiency

1) DOE must research and develop ways to improve the energy efficiency of equipment and industrial processes
2) the Environmental Protection Agency (EPA) must create a waste energy recovery program

Institutional Establishments

1) creates grants to support improved energy efficiency and sustainability at public institutions

Tax Deductions

1) $1.80/square foot for energy expenses that improve building efficiency by 50% compared to 2001 use patterns (ASHRAE 90.1)
2) system-specific deductions up to $0.60/sq. ft.

   a) interior lighting systems that are substantially lower than standard lighting requirements
   b) $0.60/sq. ft. for 40% below standard and $0.30/sq.ft. for 25% below standard
   c) a sliding scale deduction between $0.30/sq.ft. to $0.60/ sq. ft. for lighting systems that are 25%-40% more efficient

C. Proposed EPA Carbon Dioxide (CO2) Standard for New Power Plants

Consistent with the U. S. Supreme Court's decision in 2009, the Environmental Protection Agency (EPA) determined that greenhouse gas (CO2) pollution threatens Americans' health and welfare by leading to long lasting changes in our climate. These changes can have a range of negative effects on human health and the environment.

On March 27, 2012, EPA proposed a CO2 pollution standard on the construction of new power plants. The new standard does not apply to plants currently operating or new permitted plants that begin construction over the next 12 months. The standard would be flexible and would minimize CO2 pollution through the deployment of the same types of modern technologies nationwide currently employed in new power plant construction today.

For the purpose of this standard, the proposed rule would apply only to NEW fossil fuel-fired electric generating units (EGUs) larger than 25 megawatts (MW). New plants can choose to burn any fossil fuel to generate electricity for sale, including natural gas as well as coal with the appropriate technologies that reduce CO2 emissions.

The EPA is proposing that new fossil fuel power plants meet an output-based standard of 1,000 pounds of CO2 per megawatt hour (lb CO2/MWh gross). Clearly, natural gas power plants could meet this standard without any high-cost plant pollution equipment. Coal power plants, however, would be essentially prohibited due to the requirement for new CO2 pollution equipment. However, a new coal plant could still be built if it employed technology to reduce CO2 emissions to meet the standard, such as carbon capture and storage (CCS). New coal plants employing CCS would have the option to use a 30-year average of CO2 emissions to meet the proposed standard, rather than meeting the annual standard each year.

a) coal plants that install and operate CCS immediately would have the flexibility to emit more CO2 in the early years, as they learn how to best optimize the controls.

b) a utility could build a coal power plant and add CCS later,I.e., a new coal plant could be built and emit more CO2 for the first 10 years then emit less CO_2 for the next 20 years, as long as the average of those emissions meet the standard.

c) CSS technology is expected to become more widely available, which should lead to lower costs and improved performance over time.

EPA's proposed standard reflects the ongoing trend in the power sector to build cleaner plants, including new, clean burning, efficient natural gas generation, which is already the fuel of choice for most new and planned power plants.

At the same time, the standard creates a path forward for new technologies to be developed at future facilities that would allow utilities to burn coal, while emitting less CO_2 pollution.

New natural gas combined cycle (NGCC) power plant units should be able to meet the proposed standard without add-on controls. In fact, EPA estimates that 95% of the NGCC plants built since 2005 would meet the standard.

New power plants that are designed to burn coal would be able to incorporate technology to reduce CO_2 emissions to meet the standard, such as CCS. Nationwide, states like Washington, Oregon and California, currently limit CO_2 emissions. Other states, like Montana and Illinois, currently require CCS for new coal-fired power plants.

EPA also believes the standard allows flexibility to allow utilities to phase-in over tine technology to reduce CO_2. And EPA suggests that the standard is fully compatible with current utility industry investment patterns resulting in cost containment for compliance.

Thus, while it will be highly restrictive, expensive and time consuming due to the permitting process to build new coal plants in the future, it will not be entirely prohibited by the imposition of this EPA standard.

D. Climate Science

1) 650 million years ago, earth, or rodinia, was covered in ice
2) the Cambrian Explosion warmed the earth and created its atmosphere, therefore, life began 500 million years ago
3) the Cambrian Seas brought forth modern animals on earth and beneath the sea
4) the ozone layer was formed and the earth's atmosphere was created
5) 400 million years ago the earth was born or 4 billion years after the earth was formed
6) coal was formed 200 million years ago from decaying plant life
7) 300 million years ago oil and gas were formed from fossils and the earth was 4.5 billion years old
8) the Great Pangea occurred 250 million years ago with an entire earth volcanic eruption annihilating all life
9) dinosaur means terrible lizard
10) 150 million years ago the earth's current continents were formed and the earth had its first "global warming"
11) dinosaurs ruled earth 100 million years ago and produced earth's diamonds
12) 1869 diamonds found in Kimberley area of S. Africa in volcanic mines
13) Pangea split apart 100 million years ago
14) 50-65 million years ago dinosaurs disappeared
15) iridium found in space rock on earth
16) 1960 the Alvarez theory of an asteroid/meteor event killing the dinosaurs was introduced
17) 65 million years ago there was a giant meteor/asteroid strike on earth destroying the dinosaurs
18) the collision of African & European continents form the Alps, I.e., the Materhorn
19) water erosion causes the height of mountains
20) Grand Canyon formed 6 million years ago and was formed by plate tectonics
21) earth ice ages formed
22) last ice age 10,000 years ago (global warming)
23) 4.5-5 billion years ago the earth was formed and has fluctuated constantly meteorologically

24) earth is in a brief warm period between ice ages expected about 15,000 years from today

25) earth will end billions of years from now due to the end of plate tectonics

E. Global Warming Debate

There appears, as 2011 comes to an end, that there is a lack of "absolute" proof of global warming. Bjorn Lomborg, author of "Cool It" and adjunct professor at Copenhagen Business School, suggests in an Op Ed page article in the Wall St. Journal on December 12, 2011, "Global Warming and Adaptability," we look for 'adaptive' steps to deal with environmental changes as whether man's actions are the cause or not. Any carbon dioxide (CO_2) emissions reduction deal internationally by the United Nations to replace Kyoto would only have a 'negligible' impact on climate change, I.e., global warming, in coming decades. According to Lomborg, an expert in the climate debate, in order to help real people we need to focus first on 'adaptability.' Even if the world were to cut carbon emissions by 50% below 1990-levels by 2050, which is highly unlikely, the difference in temperature would be less than 0.2 degrees Fahrenheit in 2050! The world would be better served by improving crop-yield to feed the world's starving population.

In addition, Professor Henrik Svensmark, who is at the Danish National Space Institute in Copenhagen, has observed that sun spots help to control cloud cover on the earth which absorbs energy in the atmosphere from the sun causing warming and cooling cycles. This mechanism, if proven definitively, has little do with carbon emissions in our atmosphere, and is not man-made nor controllable by man.

The real problem is the science. What makes a greenhouse gas function in the role of warming the atmosphere is the ability to absorb infrared radiation, and this depends on the molecular vibrations of the molecule that allow the molecules to absorb and re-emit incident radiation. Carbon Dioxide (GO_2 weight 44), is heavier than nitrogen (NI weight 28) or oxygen (O weight 32) and those are the major gaseous components in the atmosphere, but the lighter gases, water (H_2O weight 18) or methane (CH_4 weight 16), also found in the atmosphere, are much stronger infrared absorbers by virtue of their OH and CH chemical bonds, respectively. Methane is increasing slowly but carbon dioxide is still in greater concentration in the atmosphere and is more under control of mankind than methane which results mainly from anaerobic decomposition of organic matter. Therefore, adaptability is where our focus should be, not on a 'cap and trade' tax increase policy during a deep recession in the U.S. and Europe.

F. Future Competitive Power Generation Options

There have been many studies carried out examining the economics of various future generation options, and the following are merely the most important and also focus on the nuclear element. A 2010 OECD study Projected Costs of Generating Electricity compared 2009 data for generating base-load electricity by 2015 as well as costs of power from renewables, and showed that nuclear power was very competitive at $30 per ton CO_2 cost and low discount rate. The study comprised data for 190 power plants from 17 OECD countries as well as some data from Brazil, China, Russia and South Africa. It used levelised lifetime costs with carbon price internalised (OECD only) and discounted cash flow at 5% and 10%. The precise competitiveness of different base-load technologies depended very much on local circumstances and the costs of financing and fuels.

Nuclear overnight capital costs in the OECD ranged from US$ 1556/kW for APR-1400 in South Korea through $3009 for ABWR in Japan, $3382/kW for Gen III+ in USA, $3860 for EPR at Flamanville in France to $5863/kW for EPR in Switzerland, with world median $4100/kW. Belgium, Netherlands, Czech Rep and Hungary were all over $5000/kW. In China overnight costs were $1748/kW for CPR-1000 and $2302/kW for AP1000, and in Russia $2933/kW for VVER-1150. EPRI (USA) gave $2970/kW for APWR or ABWR, Eurelectric gave $4724/kW for EPR. OECD black coal plants were costed at $807-2719/kW, those with carbon capture and compression (tabulated as CCS, but the cost not including storage) at $3223-5811/kW, brown coal $1802-3485, gas plants $635-1747/kW and onshore wind capacity $1821-3716/kW. (Overnight costs were defined here as EPC, owner's costs and contingency, but excluding interest during construction.)

OECD electricity generating cost projections for year 2010 on -5% discount rate, c/kWh					
country	nuclear	coal	coal with CCS	Gas CCGT	Onshore wind
Belgium	6.1	8.2	-	9.0	9.6
Czech R	7.0	8.5-9.4	8.8-9.3	9.2	14.6
France	5.6	-	-	-	9.0
Germany	5.0	7.0-7.9	6.8-8.5	8.5	10.6
Hungary	8.2	-	-	-	-
Japan	5.0	8.8	-	10.5	-
Korea	2.9-3.3	6.6-6.8	-	9.1	-
Netherlands	6.3	8.2	-	7.8	8.6
Slovakia	6.3	12.0	-	-	-
Switzerland	5.5-7.8	-	-	9.4	16.3
USA	4.9	7.2-7.5	6.8	7.7	4.8
China*	3.0-3.6	5.5	-	4.9	5.1-8.9
Russia*	4.3	7.5	8.7	7.1	6.3
EPRI (USA)	4.8	7.2	-	7.9	6.2
Eurelectric	6.0	6.3-7.4	7.5	8.6	11.3

*For China and Russia: 2.5c is added to coal and 1.3c to gas as carbon emission cost to enable sensible comparison with other data in those fuel/technology categories, though within those countries coal and gas will in fact be cheaper than the Table above suggests.
Source: OECD/IEA NEA 2010, table 4.1.

At 5% discount rate comparative costs are as shown above. Nuclear is comfortably cheaper than coal and gas in all countries. At 10% discount rate (below) nuclear is still cheaper than coal in all but the Eurelectric estimate and three EU countries, but in these three gas becomes cheaper still. Coal with carbon capture is mostly more expensive than either nuclear or paying the $30 per tonne for CO_2 emissions, though the report points out "great uncertainties" in the cost of projected CCS. Also, investment cost becomes a much greater proportion of power cost than with 5% discount rate.

OECD electricity generating cost projections for year 2010 on -10% discount rate, c/kWh					
country	nuclear	coal	coal with CCS	Gas CCGT	Onshore wind
Belgium	10.9	10.0	-	9.3-9.9	13.6
Czech R	11.5	11.4-13.3	13.6-14.1	10.4	21.9
France	9.2	-	-	-	12.2
Germany	8.3	8.7-9.4	9.5-11.0	9.3	14.3
Hungary	12.2	-	-	-	-
Japan	7.6	10.7	-	12.0	-
Korea	4.2-4.8	7.1-7.4	-	9.5	-
Netherlands	10.5	10.0	-	8.2	12.2
Slovakia	9.8	14.2	-	-	-
Switzerland	9.0-13.6	-	-	10.5	23.4
USA	7.7	8.8-9.3	9.4	8.3	7.0
China*	4.4-5.5	5.8	-	5.2	7.2-12.6
Russia*	6.8	9.0	11.8	7.8	9.0
EPRI (USA)	7.3	8.8	-	8.3	9.1
Eurelectric	10.6	8.0-9.0	10.2	9.4	15.5

*For China and Russia: 2.5c is added to coal and 1.3c to gas as carbon emission cost to enable sensible comparison with other data in those fuel/technology categories, though within those countries coal and gas will in fact be cheaper than the Table above suggests.
Source: OECD/IEA NEA 2010, table 4.1.

A 2004 report from the University of Chicago, funded by the US Department of Energy, compared the levelised power costs of future nuclear, coal, and gas-fired power generation in the USA. Various nuclear options were covered, and for an initial ABWR or AP1000 they range from 4.3 to 5.0 c/kWh on the basis of overnight capital costs of $1200 to $1500/kW, 60 year plant life, 5 year construction and 90% capacity. Coal gives 3.5-4.1 c/kWh and gas (CCGT) 3.5-4.5 c/kWh, depending greatly on fuel price.

The levelised nuclear power cost figures include up to 29% of the overnight capital cost as interest, and the report notes that up to another 24% of the overnight capital cost needs to be added for the initial unit of a first-of-a-kind advanced design such as the AP1000, defining the high end of the range above. For more advanced plants such as the EPR or SWR1000, overnight capital cost of $1800/kW is assumed and power costs are projected beyond the range above. However, considering a series of eight units of the same kind and assuming increased efficiency due to experience which lowers overnight capital cost, the levelised power costs drop 20% from those quoted above and where first-of-a-kind engineering costs are amortised (eg the $1500/kW case above), they drop 32%, making them competitive at about 3.4 c/kWh.

Nuclear Plant: Projected Electricity Prices (c/kWh)	
Overnight capital cost $/kW 1200 1500 1800	
First unit	7 yr build, 40 yr life
5.3	
6.2	
7.1	
	5 yr build, 60 yr life
4.3	
5.0	
5.8	
4th unit	7 yr build, 40 yr life
4.5	
4.5	
5.3	
	5 yr build, 60 yr life *
3.7	
3.7	
4.3	
8th unit	7 yr build, 40 yr life
4.2	
4.2	
4.9	
	5 yr build, 60 yr life *
3.4	
3.4	
4.0	

*calculated from above data

The study also shows that with a minimal carbon control cost impact of 1.5 c/kWh for coal and 1.0 c/kWh for gas superimposed on the above figures, nuclear is even more competitive. But more importantly it goes on to explore other policy options which would offset investment risks and compensate for first-of-a-kind engineering costs to encourage new nuclear investment, including investment tax breaks, and production tax credits phasing out after 8 years. (US wind energy gets a production tax credit which has risen to 2.1 c/kWh.)

In May 2009 an update of a heavily-referenced 2003 MIT study was published. This said that "since 2003 construction costs for all types of large-scale engineered projects have escalated dramatically. The estimated cost of constructing a nuclear power plant has increased at a rate of 15% per year heading into the current economic downturn. This is based both on the cost of actual builds in Japan and Korea and on the projected cost of new plants planned for in the United States. Capital costs for both coal and natural gas have increased as well, although not by as much. The cost of natural gas and coal that peaked sharply is now receding. Taken together, these escalating costs leave the situation [of relative costs] close to where it was in 2003." The overnight capital cost was given as $4000/kW, in 2007 dollars. Applying the same cost of capital to nuclear as to coal and gas, nuclear came out at 6.6 c/kWh, coal at 8.3 cents and gas at 7.4 cents, assuming a charge of $25/tonne CO_2 on the latter.

Escalating capital costs were also highlighted in the US Energy Information Administration (EIA) 2010 report "Updated Capital Cost Estimates for Electricity Generation Plants". The US cost estimate for new nuclear was revised upwards from $3902/kW by 37% to a value of $5339/kW for 2011 by the EIA. This is in contrast to coal, which increases by only 25%, and gas which actually shows a 3% decrease in cost. Renewables estimates show solar dropping by 25% while onshore wind increases by about 21%. The only option to increase faster than nuclear is offshore wind at 49%, while the increase in coal with CCS is about the same as nuclear. In the previous year's estimate, EIA assumed that the cost of nuclear would drop with time and experience, and that by 2030 the cost of nuclear would drop by almost 30% in constant dollars.

By way of contrast, China is stating that it expects its costs for plants under construction to come in at less than $2000/kW and that subsequent units should be in the range of $1600/kW. This estimates is for the AP1000 design, the same as used by EIA for the USA. This would mean that an AP1000 in the USA would cost about three times as much as the same plant built in China. Different labour rates in the two countries are only part of the explanation. Standardised design, numerous units being built, and increased localization are all significant factors in China.

The French Energy & Climate Directorate published in November 2008 an update of its earlier regular studies on relative electricity generating costs. This shied away from cash figures to a large extent due to rapid changes in both fuel and capital, but showed that at anything over 6000 hours production per year (68% capacity factor), nuclear was cheaper than coal or gas combined cycle (CCG). At 100% capacity CCG was 25% more expensive than nuclear. At less than 4700 hours per year CCG was cheapest, all without taking CO2 cost into account.

With the nuclear plant fixed costs were almost 75% of the total, with CCG they were less than 25% including allowance for CO2 at $20/t. Other assumptions were 8% discount rate, gas at 6.85 $/GJ, coal at EUR 60/t. The reference nuclear unit is the EPR of 1630 MWe net, sited on the coast, assuming all development costs being borne by Flamanville 3, coming on line in 2020 and operating only 40 of its planned 60 years. Capital cost apparently EUR 2000/kW. Capacity factor 91%, fuel enrichment is 5%, burnup 60 GWd/t and used fuel is reprocessed with MOX recycle. In looking at overall fuel cost, uranium at $52/lb made up about 45% of it, and even though 3% discount rate was used for back-end the study confirmed the very low cost of waste in the total—about 13% of fuel cost, mostly for reprocessing.

At the end of 2008 EdF updated the overnight cost estimate for Flamanville 3 EPR (the first French EPR, but with some supply contracts locked in before escalation) to EUR 4 billion in 2008 Euros (EUR 2434/kW), and electricity cost 5.4 cents/kWh (compared with 6.8 c/kWh for CCGT and 7.0 c/kWh for coal, "with lowest assumptions" for CO2 cost). These costs were confirmed in mid 2009, when EdF had spent nearly EUR 2 billion. In July 2010 EdF revised the overnight cost to about EUR 5 billion.

A detailed study of energy economics in Finland published in mid 2000 was important in making the strong case for additional nuclear construction there, showing that nuclear energy would be the least-cost option for new generating capacity. The study compared nuclear, coal, gas turbine combined cycle and peat. Nuclear has very much higher capital costs than the others—EUR 1749/

kW including initial fuel load, which is about three times the cost of the gas plant. But its fuel costs are much lower, and so at capacity factors above 64% it is the cheapest option.

August 2003 figures put nuclear costs at EUR 2.37 c/kWh, coal 2.81 c/kWh and natural gas at 3.23 c/kWh (on the basis of 91% capacity factor, 5% interest rate, 40 year plant life). With emission trading @ EUR 20/t CO_2, the electricity prices for coal and gas increase to 4.43 and 3.92 c/kWh respectively:

In the middle three bars of this graph the relative effects of capital and fuel costs can be clearly seen. The relatively high capital cost of nuclear power means that financing cost and time taken in construction are critical, relative to gas and even coal. But the fuel cost is very much lower, and so once a plant is built its cost of production is very much more predictable than for gas or even coal. The impact of adding a cost or carbon emissions can also be seen.

There have been a large number of recent estimates from the United States of the costs of new nuclear power plants. For example, Florida Power & Light in February 2008 released projected figures for two new AP1000 reactors at its proposed Turkey Point site. These took into account increases of some 50% in material, equipment and labour since 2004. The new figures for overnight capital cost ranged from $2444 to $3582 /kW, or when grossed up to include cooling towers, site works, land costs, transmission costs and risk management, the total cost came to $3108 to $4540 per kilowatt. Adding in finance charges almost doubled the overall figures at $5780 to $8071 / kW. FPL said that alternatives to nuclear for the plant were not economically attractive.

In May 2008 South Carolina Electric and Gas Co. and Santee Cooper locked in the price and schedule of new reactors for their Summer plant in South Carolina at $9.8 billion. (The budgeted cost earlier in the process was $10.8 billion, but some construction and material costs ended up less than projected.) The EPC contract for completing two 1,117-MW AP1000s is with Westinghouse and the Shaw Group. Beyond the cost of the actual plants, the figure includes forecast inflation and owners' costs for site preparation, contingencies and project financing. The units are expected to be in commercial operation in 2016 and 2019.

In November 2008 Duke Energy Carolinas raised the cost estimate for its Lee plant (2 x 1117 MWe AP1000) to $11 billion, excluding finance and inflation, but apparently including other owners costs.

In November 2008 TVA updated its estimates for Bellefonte units 3 & 4 for which it had submitted a COL application for twin AP1000 reactors, total 2234 MWe. It said that overnight capital cost estimates ranged from $2516 to $4649/kW for a combined construction cost of $5.6 to 10.4 billion. Total cost to the owners would be $9.9 to $17.5 billion.

Regarding bare plant costs, some recent figures apparently for overnight capital cost (or Engineering, Procurement and Construction—EPC—cost) quoted from reputable sources but not necessarily comparable are:

EdF Flamanville EPR: EUR 4 billion/$5.6 billion, so EUR 2434/kW or $3400/kW
Bruce Power Alberta 2x1100 MWe ACR, $6.2 billion, so $2800/kW
CGNPC Hongyanhe 4x1080 CPR-1000 $6.6 billion, so $1530/kW
AEO Novovronezh 6&7 2136 MWe net for $5 billion, so $2340/kW
AEP Volgodonsk 3 & 4, 2 x 1200 MWe VVER $4.8 billion, so $2000/kW
KHNP Shin Kori 3&4 1350 MWe APR-1400 for $5 billion, so $1850/kW
FPL Turkey Point 2 x 1100 MWe AP1000 $2444 to $3582/kW
Progress Energy Levy county 2 x 1105 MWe AP1000 $3462/kW
NRG South Texas 2 x 1350 MWe ABWR $8 billion, so $2900/kW
ENEC for UAE from Kepco, 4 x 1400 MWe APR-1400 $20.4 billion, so $3643/kW

A striking indication of the impact of financing costs is given by Georgia Power, which said in mid 2008 that twin 1100 MWe AP1000 reactors would cost $9.6 billion if they could be financed progressively by ratepayers, or $14 billion if not. This gives $4363 or $6360 per kilowatt including all other owners costs.

Finally, in the USA the question of whether a project is subject to regulated cost recovery or is a merchant plant is relevant, since it introduces political, financial and tactical factors. If the new build cost escalates (or is inflated), some cost recovery may be possible through higher rates can be charged by the utility if those costs are deemed prudent by the relevant regulator. By way of contrast, a merchant plant has to sell all its power competitively, so must convince its shareholders that it has a good economic case for moving forward with a new nuclear unit.

External costs

The report of a major European study of the external costs of various fuel cycles, focusing on coal and nuclear, was released in mid 2001—ExternE. It shows that in clear cash terms nuclear energy incurs about one tenth of the costs of coal. The external costs are defined as those actually incurred in relation to health and the environment and quantifiable but not built into the cost of the electricity. If these costs were in fact included, the EU price of electricity from coal would double and that from gas would increase 30%. These are without attempting to include the external costs of global warming.

The European Commission launched the project in 1991 in collaboration with the US Department of Energy, and it was the first research project of its kind "to put plausible financial figures against damage resulting from different forms of electricity production for the entire EU". The methodology considers emissions, dispersion and ultimate impact. With nuclear energy the risk of accidents is factored in along with high estimates of radiological impacts from mine tailings (waste management and decommissioning being already within the cost to the consumer). Nuclear energy averages 0.4 euro cents/kWh, much the same as hydro, coal is over 4.0 cents (4.1-7.3), gas ranges 1.3-2.3 cents and only wind shows up better than nuclear, at 0.1-0.2 cents/kWh average. NB these are the external costs only.

Sources:
OECD/ IEA NEA 2010, Projected Costs of Generating Electricity.
OECD, 1994, The Economics of the Nuclear Fuel Cycle.
NEI: US generating cost data.
Tarjanne, R & Rissanen, S, 2000, Nuclear Power: Lest-cost option
for baseload electricity in Finland; in Proceedings 25th International
Symposium, Uranium Institute.
Gutierrez, J 2003, Nuclear Fuel—key for the competitiveness of nuclear
energy in Spain, WNA Symposium.
University of Chicago, August 2004, The Economic Future of Nuclear
Power.

Nuclear Energy Institute, August 2008, The cost of new generating capacity in perspective.

G. Peak Electricity Capacity in US Is Supply Constrained

H. Nuclear Power Plants Are Prohibited from Populated Areas

I. 10-15 Year Construction Lead-Times for Nuclear Power Plants

J. Strict State Reliability Standards Enforced Nationwide for Nuclear Power Plants

K. Nuclear Plant Capital Costs Are 25%-37% More Expensive Than Natural Gas

L. Coal Plant CO2 Restrictions due to Clean Air Act Provisions

M. Vast Natural Gas Pipeline Network Throughout U.S.

N. Ample Natural Gas Supply in Shale Formations Domestically (TX, LA, PA, NY)

O. Nuclear Waste Storage and Transportation Are Problematic (Environmentally, National Security, Safety, etc,)

P. Electricity Capacity Enhancements

1) high-efficiency equipment
2) shifting load off peak
3) smart metering
4) time-of-use pricing
5) renewable resources (solar, wind, geothermal, tidal)

Q. "Capital Cost Advantage: Natural Gas v. Nuclear Electric Generation"

While nuclear electric generation has been tauted by the nuclear industry as the panacea for building new power generation capacity, desperately needed in the United States today, the economics do not bear that opinion out. To begin with, nuclear plant capital costs are some 25%-37% more expensive than comparable natural gas-fired power generation.

In addition, from a purely environmental perspective, natural gas produces 28 watts of electricity per square meter of land used to drill a standard natural gas well. While it is true that nuclear plant power generation produces a larger amount of watts per square meter, I.e., about 2,000 watts, this is dwarfed by the significant capital cost disadvantage.

The first expansion of a nuclear power plant since the 1970s was approved for construction recently in Georgia by the Southern Company for expected completion in 2014. The 100-plus nuclear plants operating in the U. S. currently provide 20% of the U.S. electricity capacity. Cost overruns and safety concerns following the 1979 Three Mile Island accident stalled new construction. In fact, even this recent approval in Georgia of a permit by the Nuclear Regulatory Commission (NRC) was not without controversy. The NRC Chairman, Gregory Jaczko, opposed the Vogtle plant. He proposed that a condition be included in the permit that before operating the two reactors, Southern should follow any forthcoming safety enhancements put forward by the NRC as it reviews the meltdown last year at Japan's Fukushima Daiichi nuclear power plant. In addition, Southern needs a federal loan guarantee to help finance the $14 billion project, which it will operate and co-own with three other partners.

The outlook for additional nuclear plants in the near term isn't promising either because of low electricity demand resulting from the deep recession and the sharp decline in natural gas prices, the main competing fuel to nuclear power generation. The Vogtle reators and a pair of South Carolina reactors will surely be the only facilities built in the U.S. before 2020.

In fact, existing nuclear facilities are facing questions on their safety. The San Onofre Nuclear Generating Station in southern California has been shut down due to deteriorating steam pipes in both reactors. This development has heightened public concern in California, specifically, but it is echoed nationwide, to permanently close the plant cutting-off 2,200 megawatts of generating capacity in an already tight electricity capacity environment. This situation will only worsen in the near-term future as nuclear plants are retired and not replaced.

Nuclear power is cost competitive with other forms of electricity generation, except where there is direct access to low-cost fossil fuels.

Fuel costs for nuclear plants are a minor proportion of total generating costs, though capital costs are greater than those for coal-fired plants and much greater than those for gas-fired plants. In assessing the economics of nuclear power, decommissioning and waste disposal costs are fully taken into account.

Assessing the relative costs of new generating plants utilising different technologies is a complex matter and the results depend crucially on location. Coal is, and will probably remain, economically attractive in countries such as China, the USA and Australia with abundant and accessible domestic coal resources as long as carbon emissions are cost-free. Gas is also competitive for base-load power in many places, particularly using combined-cycle plants, especially ad gas prices have remained low giving gas generation a competitive advantage.

Assessing the relative costs of new generating plants utilising different technologies is a complex matter and the results depend crucially on location. Coal is, and will probably remain, economically attractive in countries such as China, the USA and Australia with abundant and accessible domestic coal resources as long as carbon emissions are cost-free. Gas is also competitive for base-load power in many places, particularly using combined-cycle plants, though rising gas prices have removed much of the advantage.

Nuclear energy is, in many places, particularly the developing world, competitive with fossil fuels for electricity generation, despite relatively high capital costs and the need to internalise all waste disposal and decommissioning costs. If the social, health and environmental costs of fossil fuels are also taken into account, the economics of nuclear power are suspect, at best.

R. The Economics of Nuclear Power

Nuclear power is cost competitive with other forms of electricity generation, except where there is direct access to low-cost fossil fuels.

Fuel costs for nuclear plants are a minor proportion of total generating costs, though capital costs are greater than those for coal-fired plants and much greater than those for gas-fired plants. In assessing the economics of nuclear power, decommissioning and waste disposal costs are fully taken into account.

Assessing the relative costs of new generating plants utilising different technologies is a complex matter and the results depend crucially on location. Coal is, and will probably remain, economically attractive in countries such as China, the USA and Australia with abundant and accessible domestic coal resources as long as carbon emissions are cost-free. Gas is also competitive for base-load power in many places, particularly using combined-cycle plants, because gas prices have remained low.

Nuclear energy is, in many places, competitive with fossil fuels for electricity generation, despite relatively high capital costs and the need to internalise all waste disposal and decommissioning costs. If the social, health and environmental costs of fossil fuels are also taken into account, the economics of nuclear power are outstanding.

S. The New Economics of Nuclear Power

From the outset, the basic attraction of nuclear energy has been its low fuel costs compared with coal, oil and gas-fired plants. Uranium, however, has to be processed, enriched and fabricated into fuel elements, and about half of the cost is due to enrichment and fabrication. In the assessment of the economics of nuclear power allowances must also be made for the management of radioactive used fuel and the ultimate disposal of this used fuel or the wastes separated from it. But even with these included, the total fuel costs of a nuclear power plant in the OECD are typically about a third of those for a coal-fired plant and between a quarter and a fifth of those for a gas combined-cycle plant. The US Nuclear Energy Institute suggests that for a coal-fired plant 78% of the cost is the fuel, for a gas-fired plant the figure is 89%, and for nuclear the uranium is about 14%, or double that to include all front end costs.

In March 2011, the approx. US $ cost to get 1 kg of uranium as UO2 reactor fuel (at current spot uranium price):

Uranium:	8.9 kg U3O8 x $146	US$ 1300
Conversion:	7.5 kg U x $13	US$ 98
Enrichment:	7.3 SWU x $155	US$ 1132
Fuel fabrication:	per kg	US$ 240
Total, approx:		US$ 2770

At 45,000 MWd/t burn-up this gives 360,000 kWh electrical per kg, hence fuel cost: 0.77 c/kWh. Fuel costs are one area of steadily increasing efficiency and cost reduction. For instance, in Spain the nuclear electricity cost was reduced by 29% over 1995-2001. This involved boosting enrichment levels and burn-up to achieve 40% fuel cost reduction. Prospectively, a further 8% increase in burn-up will give another 5% reduction in fuel cost.

Uranium has the advantage of being a highly concentrated source of energy which is easily and cheaply transportable. The quantities needed are very much less than for coal or oil. One kilogram of natural uranium will yield about 20,000 times as much energy as the same amount of coal. It is therefore intrinsically a very portable and tradeable commodity.

The fuel's contribution to the overall cost of the electricity produced is relatively small, so even a large fuel price escalation will have relatively little effect (see below). Uranium is abundant. There are other possible savings. For example, if used fuel is reprocessed and the recovered plutonium and uranium is used in mixed oxide (MOX) fuel, more energy can be extracted. The costs of achieving this are large, but are offset by MOX fuel not needing enrichment and particularly by the smaller amount of high-level wastes produced at the end. Seven UO2 fuel assemblies give rise to one MOX assembly plus some vitrified high-level waste, resulting in only about 35% of the volume, mass and cost of disposal.

T. Comparing the Economics of Electricity Generation

It is important to distinguish between the economics of nuclear plants already in operation and those at the planning stage. Once capital investment costs re effectively "sunk", existing plants operate at very low costs and are effectively "cash machines". Their operations and maintenance (O&M) and fuel costs (including used fuel management) are, along with hydropower plants, at the low end of the spectrum and make them very suitable as base-load power suppliers. This is irrespective of whether the investment costs are amortized or depreciated in corporate financial accounts—assuming the forward or marginal costs of operation are below the power price, the plant will operate. US figures for 2008 published by NEI show the general picture, with nuclear generating power at 1.87 c/kW.o

Note: the above data refer to fuel plus operation and maintenance costs only, they exclude capital, since this varies greatly among utilities and states, as well as with the age of the plant. A Finnish study in 2000 also quantified fuel price sensitivity to electricity costs:

These show that a doubling of fuel prices would result in the electricity cost for nuclear rising about 9%, for coal rising 31% and for gas 66%. Gas prices have since risen significantly. The impact of varying the uranium price in isolation is shown below in a worked example of a typical US plant, assuming no alteration in the tails assay at the enrichment plant.

Doubling the uranium price (say from $25 to $50 per lb U3O8) takes the fuel cost up from 0.50 to 0.62 US cents per kWh, an increase of one quarter, and the expected cost of generation of the best US plants from 1.3 US cents per kWh to 1.42 cents per kWh (an increase of almost 10%). So while there is some impact, it is comparatively minor, especially by comparison with the impact of gas prices on the economics of gas generating plants. In these, 90% of the marginal costs can be fuel. Only if uranium prices rise to above $100 per lb U3O8 ($260 /kgU) and stay there for a prolonged period (which seems very unlikely) will the impact on nuclear generating costs be considerable.

Nevertheless, for nuclear power plants operating in competitive power markets where it is impossible to pass on any fuel price increases (ie the utility is a price-taker), higher uranium prices will cut corporate profitability. Yet fuel costs have been relatively stable over time—the rise in the world uranium price between 2003 and 2007 added to generation costs, but conversion, enrichment and fuel fabrication costs did not followed the same trend.

For prospective new nuclear plants, the fuel element is even less significant (see below). The typical front end nuclear fuel cost is typically only 15-20% of the total, as opposed to 30-40% for operating nuclear plants.

Understanding the cost of new generating capacity and its output requires careful analysis of what is in any set of figures. There are three broad components: capital, finance and operating costs. Capital and financing costs make up the project cost.

Capital costs comprise several things: the bare plant cost (usually identified as engineering-procurement-construction—EPC—cost), the owner's costs (land, cooling infrastructure, administration and associated buildings, site works, switchyards, project management, licences, etc), cost escalation and inflation. Owner's costs may include transmission infrastructure. The term "overnight capital cost" is often used, meaning EPC plus owners' costs and excluding financing, escalation due to increased material and labour costs, and inflation. Construction cost—sometimes called "all-in cost", adds to overnight cost any escalation and interest during construction and up to the start of construction. It is expressed in the same units as overnight cost and is useful for identifying the total cost of construction and for determining the effects of construction delays. In general the construction costs of nuclear power plants are significantly higher than for coal—or gas-fired plants because of the need to use special materials, and to incorporate sophisticated safety features and back-up control equipment. These contribute much of the nuclear generation cost, but once the plant is built the cost variables are minor.

Long construction periods will push up financing costs, and in the past they have done so spectacularly. In Asia construction times have tended to be shorter, for instance the new-generation 1300 MWe Japanese reactors which began operating in 1996 and 1997 were built in a little over four years, and 48 to 54 months is typical projection for plants today.

Decommissioning costs are about 9-15% of the initial capital cost of a nuclear power plant. But when discounted, they contribute only a few percent to the investment cost and even less to the generation cost. In the USA they account for 0.1-0.2 cent/kWh, which is no more than 5% of the cost of the electricity produced.

Financing costs will depend on the rate of interest on debt, the debt-equity ratio, and if it is regulated, how the capital costs are recovered. There must also be an allowance for a rate of return on equity, which is risk capital.

Operating costs include operating and maintenance (O&M) plus fuel. Fuel cost figures include used fuel management and final waste disposal. These costs, while usually external for other technologies, are internal for nuclear power (ie they have to be paid or set aside securely by the utility generating the power, and the cost passed on to the customer in the actual tariff). This "back-end" of the fuel cycle, including used fuel storage or disposal in a waste repository, contributes up to 10% of the overall costs per kWh,—rather less if there is direct disposal of used fuel rather than reprocessing. The $26 billion US used fuel program is funded by a 0.1 cent/kWh levy.

Calculations of relative generating costs are made using levelised costs, meaning average costs of producing electricity including capital, finance, owner's costs on site, fuel and operation over a plant's lifetime, with provision for decommissioning and waste disposal. It is important to note that capital cost figures quoted by reactor vendors, or which are general and not site-specific, will usually just be for EPC costs. This is because owner's costs will vary hugely, most of all according to whether a plant is Greenfield or at an established site, perhaps replacing an old plant.

Mid 2008 vendor figures for overnight costs (excluding owner's costs) have been quoted as:
GE-Hitachi ESBWR just under $3000/kW
GE-Hitachi ABWR just over $3000/kW
Westinghouse AP1000 about $3000/kW

There are several possible sources of variation which preclude confident comparison of overnight or EPC (Engineering, Procurement & Construction) capital costs—eg whether initial core load of fuel is included. Much more obvious is whether the price is for the nuclear island alone (Nuclear Steam Supply System) or the whole plant including turbines and generators—all the above figures include these. Further differences relate to site works such as cooling towers as well as land and permitting—usually they are all owner's costs as outlined earlier in this section. Financing costs are additional, adding typically around 30%, and finally there is the question of whether cost figures are in current (or specified year) dollar values.

There have been many studies carried out examining the economics of various future generation options, and the following are merely the most important and also focus on the nuclear element. A 2010 OECD study Projected Costs of generating Electricity compared 2009 data for generating base-load electricity by 2015 as well as costs of power from renewables, and showed that nuclear power was very competitive at $30 per tonne CO2 cost and low discount rate. The study comprised data for 190 power plants from 17 OECD countries as well as some data from Brazil, China, Russia and South Africa. It used levelised lifetime costs with carbon price internalised (OECD only) and discounted cash flow at 5% and 10%, as previously. The precise competitiveness of different base-load technologies depended very much on local circumstances and the costs of financing and fuels.

Nuclear overnight capital costs in OECD ranged from US$ 1556/kW for APR-1400 in South Korea through $3009 for ABWR in Japan, $3382/kW for Gen III+ in USA, $3860 for EPR at Flamanville in France to $5863/kW for EPR in Switzerland, with world median $4100/kW. Belgium, Netherlands, Czech Rep and Hungary were all over $5000/kW. In China overnight costs were $1748/kW for CPR-1000 and $2302/kW for AP1000, and in Russia $2933/kW for VVER-1150. EPRI (USA) gave $2970/kW for APWR or ABWR, Eurelectric gave $4724/kW for EPR. OECD black coal plants were costed at $807-2719/kW, those with carbon capture and compression (tabulated as CCS, but the cost not including storage) at $3223-5811/kW, brown coal $1802-3485, gas plants $635-1747/kW and onshore wind capacity $1821-3716/kW. (Overnight costs were defined here as EPC, owner's costs and contingency, but excluding interest during construction.)

OECD electricity generating cost projections for year 2010 on -5% discount rate, c/kWh					
country	nuclear	coal	coal with CCS	Gas CCGT	Onshore wind
Belgium	6.1	8.2	-	9.0	9.6
Czech R	7.0	8.5-9.4	8.8-9.3	9.2	14.6
France	5.6	-	-	-	9.0
Germany	5.0	7.0-7.9	6.8-8.5	8.5	10.6
Hungary	8.2	-	-	-	-
Japan	5.0	8.8	-	10.5	-
Korea	2.9-3.3	6.6-6.8	-	9.1	-
Netherlands	6.3	8.2	-	7.8	8.6
Slovakia	6.3	12.0	-	-	-
Switzerland	5.5-7.8	-	-	9.4	16.3
USA	4.9	7.2-7.5	6.8	7.7	4.8
China*	3.0-3.6	5.5	-	4.9	5.1-8.9
Russia*	4.3	7.5	8.7	7.1	6.3
EPRI (USA)	4.8	7.2	-	7.9	6.2
Eurelectric	6.0	6.3-7.4	7.5	8.6	11.3

*For China and Russia: 2.5c is added to coal and 1.3c to gas as carbon emission cost to enable sensible comparison with other data in those fuel/technology categories, though within those countries coal and gas will in fact be cheaper than the Table above suggests.

Source: OECD/IEA NEA 2010, table 4.1.

At 5% discount rate comparative costs are as shown above. Nuclear is comfortably cheaper than coal and gas in all countries. At 10% discount rate (below) nuclear is still cheaper than coal in all but the Eurelectric estimate and three EU countries, but in these three gas becomes cheaper still. Coal with carbon capture is mostly more expensive than either nuclear or paying the $30 per tonne for CO2 emissions, though the report points out "great uncertainties" in the cost of projected CCS. Also, investment cost becomes a much greater proportion of power cost than with 5% discount rate.

OECD electricity generating cost projections for year 2010 on -10% discount rate, c/kWh					
country	nuclear	coal	coal with CCS	Gas CCGT	Onshore wind
Belgium	10.9	10.0	-	9.3-9.9	13.6
Czech R	11.5	11.4-13.3	13.6-14.1	10.4	21.9
France	9.2	-	-	-	12.2
Germany	8.3	8.7-9.4	9.5-11.0	9.3	14.3
Hungary	12.2	-	-	-	-
Japan	7.6	10.7	-	12.0	-
Korea	4.2-4.8	7.1-7.4	-	9.5	-
Netherlands	10.5	10.0	-	8.2	12.2
Slovakia	9.8	14.2	-	-	-
Switzerland	9.0-13.6	-	-	10.5	23.4
USA	7.7	8.8-9.3	9.4	8.3	7.0
China*	4.4-5.5	5.8	-	5.2	7.2-12.6
Russia*	6.8	9.0	11.8	7.8	9.0
EPRI (USA)	7.3	8.8	-	8.3	9.1
Eurelectric	10.6	8.0-9.0	10.2	9.4	15.5

*For China and Russia: 2.5c is added to coal and 1.3c to gas as carbon emission cost to enable sensible comparison with other data in those fuel/technology categories, though within those countries coal and gas will in fact be cheaper than the Table above suggests.
Source: OECD/IEA NEA 2010, table 4.1.

A 2004 report from the University of Chicago, funded by the US Department of Energy, compared the levelised power costs of future nuclear, coal, and gas-fired power generation in the USA. Various nuclear options were covered, and for an initial ABWR or AP1000 they range from 4.3 to 5.0 c/kWh on the basis of overnight capital costs of $1200 to $1500/kW, 60 year plant life, 5 year construction and 90% capacity. Coal gives 3.5 - 4.1 c/kWh and gas (CCGT) 3.5 - 4.5 c/kWh, depending greatly on fuel price.

The levelised nuclear power cost figures include up to 29% of the overnight capital cost as interest, and the report notes that up to another 24% of the overnight capital cost needs to be added for the initial unit of a first-of-a-kind advanced design such as the AP1000, defining the high end of the range above. For more advanced plants such as the EPR or SWR1000, overnight capital cost of $1800/kW is assumed and power costs are projected beyond the range above. However, considering a series of eight units of the same kind and assuming increased efficiency due to experience which lowers overnight capital cost, the levelised power costs drop 20% from those quoted above and where first-of-a-kind engineering costs are amortised (eg the $1500/kW case above), they drop 32%, making them competitive at about 3.4 c/kWh.

Nuclear Plant: Projected Electricity Costs (c/kWh)	
Overnight capital cost $/kW 1200 1500 1800	
First unit	7 yr build, 40 yr life
5.3	
6.2	
7.1	
	5 yr build, 60 yr life
4.3	
5.0	
5.8	
4th unit	7 yr build, 40 yr life
4.5	
4.5	
5.3	
	5 yr build, 60 yr life *
3.7	
3.7	
4.3	
8th unit	7 yr build, 40 yr life
4.2	
4.2	
4.9	
	5 yr build, 60 yr life *
3.4	
3.4	
4.0	

*calculated from above data

The study also shows that with a minimal carbon control cost impact of 1.5 c/kWh for coal and 1.0 c/kWh for gas superimposed on the above figures, nuclear is even more competitive. But more importantly it goes on to explore other policy options which would offset investment risks and compensate for first-of-a-kind engineering costs to encourage new nuclear investment, including investment tax breaks, and production tax credits phasing out after 8 years. (US wind energy gets a production tax credit which has risen to 2.1 c/kWh.)

In May 2009 an update of a heavily-referenced 2003 MIT study was published. This said that "since 2003 construction costs for all types of large-scale engineered projects have escalated dramatically. The estimated cost of constructing a nuclear power plant has increased at a rate of 15% per year heading into the current economic downturn. This is based both on the cost of actual builds in Japan and Korea and on the projected cost of new plants planned for in the United States. Capital costs for both coal and natural gas have increased as well, although not by as much. The cost of natural gas and coal that peaked sharply is now receding. Taken together, these escalating costs leave the situation [of relative costs] close to where it was in 2003." The overnight capital cost was given as $4000/kW, in 2007 dollars. Applying the same cost of capital to nuclear as to coal and gas, nuclear came out at 6.6 c/kWh, coal at 8.3 cents and gas at 7.4 cents, assuming a charge of $25/tonne CO_2 on the latter.

Escalating capital costs were also highlighted in the US Energy Information Administration (EIA) 2010 report "Updated Capital Cost Estimates for Electricity Generation Plants". The US cost estimate for new nuclear was revised upwards from $3902/kW by 37% to a value of $5339/kW for 2011 by the EIA. This is in contrast to coal, which increases by only 25%, and gas which actually shows a 3% decrease in cost. Renewables estimates show solar dropping by 25% while onshore wind increases by about 21%. The only option to increase faster than nuclear is offshore wind at 49%, while the increase in coal with CCS is about the same as nuclear. In the previous year's estimate, EIA assumed that the cost of nuclear would drop with time and experience, and that by 2030 the cost of nuclear would drop by almost 30% in constant dollars.

By way of contrast, China is stating that it expects its costs for plants under construction to come in at less than $2000/kW and that subsequent units should be in the range of $1600/kW. This estimates is for the AP1000 design, the same as used by EIA for the USA. This would mean that an AP1000 in the USA would cost about three times as much as the same plant built in China. Different labour rates in the two countries are only part of the explanation. Standardised design, numerous units being built, and increased localization are all significant factors in China.

The French Energy & Climate Directorate published in November 2008 an update of its earlier regular studies on relative electricity generating costs. This shied away from cash figures to a large extent due to rapid changes in both fuel and capital, but showed that at anything over 6000 hours production per year (68% capacity factor), nuclear was cheaper than coal or gas combined cycle (CCG). At 100% capacity CCG was 25% more expensive than nuclear. At less than 4700 hours per year CCG was cheapest, all without taking CO_2 cost into account.

With the nuclear plant fixed costs were almost 75% of the total, with CCG they were less than 25% including allowance for CO_2 at $20/t. Other assumptions were 8% discount rate, gas at 6.85 $/GJ, coal at EUR 60/t. The reference nuclear unit is the EPR of 1630 MWe net, sited on the coast, assuming all development costs being borne by Flamanville 3, coming on line in 2020 and operating only 40 of its planned 60 years. Capital cost apparently EUR 2000/kW. Capacity factor 91%, fuel enrichment is 5%, burnup 60 GWd/t and used fuel is reprocessed with MOX recycle. In looking at overall fuel cost, uranium at $52/lb made up about 45% of it, and even though 3% discount rate was used for back-end the study confirmed the very low cost of waste in the total—about 13% of fuel cost, mostly for reprocessing.

At the end of 2008 EdF updated the overnight cost estimate for Flamanville 3 EPR (the first French EPR, but with some supply contracts locked in before escalation) to EUR 4 billion in 2008 Euros (EUR 2434/kW), and electricity cost 5.4 cents/kWh (compared with 6.8 c/kWh for CCGT and 7.0 c/kWh for coal, "with lowest assumptions" for CO_2 cost). These costs were confirmed in mid 2009, when EdF had spent nearly EUR 2 billion. In July 2010 EdF revised the overnight cost to about EUR 5 billion.

A detailed study of energy economics in Finland published in mid 2000 was important in making the strong case for additional nuclear construction there, showing that nuclear energy would be the least-cost option for new generating capacity. The study compared nuclear, coal, gas turbine combined cycle and peat. Nuclear has very much higher capital costs than the others—EUR 1749/kW including initial fuel load, which is about three times the cost of the gas plant. But its fuel costs are much lower, and so at capacity factors above 64% it is the cheapest option.

August 2003 figures put nuclear costs at EUR 2.37 c/kWh, coal 2.81 c/kWh and natural gas at 3.23 c/kWh (on the basis of 91% capacity factor, 5% interest rate, 40 year plant life). With emission trading @ EUR 20/t CO_2, the electricity prices for coal and gas increase to 4.43 and 3.92 c/kWh respectively:

In the middle three bars of this graph the relative effects of capital and fuel costs can be clearly seen. The relatively high capital cost of nuclear power means that financing cost and time taken in construction are critical, relative to gas and even coal. But the fuel cost is very much lower, and so once a plant is built its cost of production is very much more predictable than for gas or even coal. The impact of adding a cost or carbon emissions can also be seen.

There have been a large number of recent estimates from the United States of the costs of new nuclear power plants. For example, Florida Power & Light in February 2008 released projected figures for two new AP1000 reactors at its proposed Turkey Point site. These took into account increases of some 50% in material, equipment and labour since 2004. The new figures for overnight capital cost ranged from $2444 to $3582 /kW, or when grossed up to include cooling towers, site works, land costs, transmission costs and risk management, the total cost came to $3108 to $4540 per kilowatt. Adding in finance charges almost doubled the overall figures at $5780 to $8071 /kW. FPL said that alternatives to nuclear for the plant were not economically attractive.

In May 2008 South Carolina Electric and Gas Co. and Santee Cooper locked in the price and schedule of new reactors for their Summer plant in South Carolina at $9.8 billion. (The budgeted cost earlier in the process was $10.8 billion, but some construction and material costs ended up less than projected.) The EPC contract for completing two 1,117-MW AP1000s is with Westinghouse and the Shaw Group. Beyond the cost of the actual plants, the figure includes forecast inflation and owners' costs for site preparation, contingencies and project financing. The units are expected to be in commercial operation in 2016 and 2019. In November 2008 Duke Energy Carolinas raised the cost estimate for its Lee plant (2 x 1117 MWe AP1000) to $11 billion, excluding finance and inflation, but apparently including other owners costs.

In November 2008 TVA updated its estimates for Bellefonte units 3 & 4 for which it had submitted a COL application for twin AP1000 reactors, total 2234 MWe. It said that overnight capital cost estimates ranged from $2516 to $4649/kW for a combined construction cost of $5.6 to 10.4 billion. Total cost to the owners would be $9.9 to $17.5 billion.

Regarding bare plant costs, some recent figures apparently for overnight capital cost (or Engineering, Procurement and Construction—EPC—cost) quoted from reputable sources but not necessarily comparable are:

EdF Flamanville EPR: EUR 4 billion/$5.6 billion, so EUR 2434/kW or $3400/kW
Bruce Power Alberta 2x1100 MWe ACR, $6.2 billion, so $2800/kW
CGNPC Hongyanhe 4x1080 CPR-1000 $6.6 billion, so $1530/kW
AEO Novovronezh 6&7 2136 MWe net for $5 billion, so $2340/kW
AEP Volgodonsk 3 & 4, 2 x 1200 MWe VVER $4.8 billion, so $2000/kW
KHNP Shin Kori 3&4 1350 MWe APR-1400 for $5 billion, so $1850/kW
FPL Turkey Point 2 x 1100 MWe AP1000 $2444 to $3582/kW
Progress Energy Levy county 2 x 1105 MWe AP1000 $3462/kW
NRG South Texas 2 x 1350 MWe ABWR $8 billion, so $2900/kW
ENEC for UAE from Kepco, 4 x 1400 MWe APR-1400 $20.4 billion, so $3643/kW

A striking indication of the impact of financing costs is given by Georgia Power, which said in mid 2008 that twin 1100 MWe AP1000 reactors would cost $9.6 billion if they could be financed progressively by ratepayers, or $14 billion if not. This gives $4363 or $6360 per kilowatt including all other owners costs.

Finally, in the USA the question of whether a project is subject to regulated cost recovery or is a merchant plant is relevant, since it introduces political, financial and tactical factors. If the new build cost escalates (or is inflated), some cost recovery may be possible through higher rates can be charged by the utility if those costs are deemed prudent by the relevant regulator. By way of contrast, a merchant plant has to sell all its power competitively, so must convince its shareholders that it has a good economic case for moving forward with a new nuclear unit.

External costs

The report of a major European study of the external costs of various fuel cycles, focusing on coal and nuclear, was released in mid 2001—ExternE. It shows that in clear cash terms nuclear energy incurs about one tenth of the costs of coal. The external costs are defined as those actually incurred in relation to health and the environment and quantifiable but not built into the cost of the electricity. If these costs were in fact included, the EU price of electricity from coal would double and that from gas would increase 30%. These are without attempting to include the external costs of global warming.

The European Commission launched the project in 1991 in collaboration with the US Department of Energy, and it was the first research project of its kind "to put plausible financial figures against damage resulting from different forms of electricity production for the entire EU". The methodology considers emissions, dispersion and ultimate impact. With nuclear energy the risk of accidents is factored in along with high estimates of radiological impacts from mine tailings (waste management and decommissioning being already within the cost to the consumer). Nuclear energy averages 0.4 euro cents/kWh, much the same as hydro, coal is over 4.0 cents (4.1-7.3), gas ranges 1.3-2.3 cents and only wind shows up better than nuclear, at 0.1-0.2 cents/kWh average. NB these are the external costs only.

Projected Costs of Generating Electricity.
OECD, 1994, The Economics of the Nuclear Fuel Cycle.
NEI: US generating cost data.
Tarjanne, R & Rissanen, S, 2000, Nuclear Power: Lest-cost option for baseload electricity in Finland; in Proceedings 25th International Symposium, Uranium Institute.
Gutierrez, J 2003, Nuclear Fuel—key for the competitiveness of nuclear energy in Spain, WNA Symposium.

University of Chicago, August 2004, The Economic Future of Nuclear Power.

Nuclear Energy Institute, August 2008, The cost of new generating capacity is highly competitive.

Peak Electricity Capacity in US Is Supply

Constrained

Nuclear Power Plants

Are Prohibited from

Populated Areas

10-15 Year Construction Lead-Times for Nuclear

Power Plants

Strict State Reliability Standards Enforced Nationwide for Power Plants

Nuclear Plant Capital Costs Are 25%-37% More Expensive Than Natural Gas

Coal Plant Carbon Dioxide (CO2) Restrictions due to Clean Air Act

Provisions

Vast Natural Gas

Pipeline Network

Throughout U.S.

Ample Natural Gas Supply in Shale Formations Domestically (TX, LA, PA, NY) through Horizontal Drilling and Fracting

Nuclear Waste Storage and

Transportation Are Problematic (Environmentally, National Security, etc.)

Enhanced Electricity Capacity Techniques

1) high-efficiency equipment
2) shifting load off peak
3) smart metering
4) time-of-use pricing
5) renewable resources (solar, wind, geothermal, tidal)

U. Recent Developments: Energy Policy Legislation and Climate Change

Energy Policy Legislation

1. Energy Independence and Security Act of 2007 (EPAct 2007) additional rules: the stated purpose of the Act is "to move the United States toward greater energy independence and security, to increase the production of

clean renewable fuels, to protect consumers, to increase the efficiency of products, buildings,and vehicles, to promote research on and deploy greenhouse gas capture and storage options, and to improve the energy performance of the Federal Government, and other purposes."

This Act was signed into law in December, 2007 and changed U.S. energy policy, as well as promoted the reduction of CO_2 emissions contributing to global warming, in the following ways:

a) increased Corporate Average Fuel Economy (CAFE) standards. Automakers are required to boost fleetwide gasoline mileage to 35 mpg by 2020. This applies to all passenger automobiles, including light trucks. Manufacturers can receive a credit in one vehicle class if mpg exceeds the CAFE standards.

b) improved vehicle technology for the development of plug-in hybrid electric vehicles. The federal government must establish a loan program for advanced battery technology and develop incentives for fleet buying of heavy-duty hybrid vehicles.

c) new efficiency standards for federal fleets which must meet new low greenhouse gas emission standards. Using 2005 as a base year, by 2015 federal agencies must reduce petroleum consumption by 20% and increase the use of alternative fuel by 10% yearly.

d) renewable fuel standards to include taxpayer funding for increased production of biofuels and an increase to 36 billion gallons of total gasoline additives in biofuels by 2022. In addition, 21 billion gallons of the 2022 biofuels total must be derived from non-cornstarch products. The Scretary of Energy must initiate studies on the use of algae as a feedstock for biofuels and the improved performance of engines with the use if biodiesel.

e) biofuels research and development grants for states with low biomass ethanol production

f) appliance efficiency improvements for external power supplies, in-home appliances, electrical motors, residential boilers and HVAC equipment

g) lighting efficiency upgrades requiring 25% greater efficiency for light bulbs, phased-in from 2012 through 2014, thereby eliminating the production and importation of incandescent light bulbs. Exemptions for bulbs less tha 50 watts and greater than 150 watts. Essentially, a 200% greater efficiency for light light bulbs by 2020

h) residential building efficiency standards
i) high-performance commercial buildings aims to create a nationwide zero-net-energy initiative for commercial buildings constructed after 2025 while those built before 2025 should meet the initiative by 2050
j) high-performance federal buildings requires all lighting in federal buildings to use Energy Star products. New and renovated federal buildings must reduce fossil fuel consumption by 55% from 2003 levels by 2015 and 80% by 2020, while new federal buildings must be carbon-neutral by 2030
k) industrial efficiency increases
l) high-performance schools
m) public institutional efficiency
n) public & assisted housing efficiency standards
o) general provisions

    1) $10,000,000 fund for DOE to support one federal project each year for five years
    2) $10,000,000 fund set aside by DOE to support four projects at universities over five years

2. Climate Change

Global Warming Debate

There appears, as 2011 comes to an end, that there is a lack of "absolute" proof of global warming. Bjorn Lomborg, author of "Cool It" and adjunct professor at Copenhagen Business School, suggests in an Op Ed page article in the Wall St. Journal on December 12, 2011, "Global Warming and Adaptability," we look for 'adaptive' steps to deal with environmental changes as common sense (and is the premise of this book) whether man's actions are the cause or not. Any carbon dioxide (CO_2) emissions reduction deal internationally by the United Nations at Durbin to replace Kyoto would only have a 'negligible' impact on climate change, I.e., global warming, in coming decades. According to Lomborg, an expert in the climate debate, in order to help real people we need to focus first on 'adaptability.' Even if the world were to cut carbon emissions by 50% below 1990-levels by 2050, which is highly unlikely, the difference in temperature would be less than 0.2 degrees Fahrenheit in 2050! The world would be better served by improving crop-yield to feed the world's starving population.

In addition, Professor Henrik Svensmark, who is at the Danish National Space Institute in Copenhagen, has observed that sun spots help to control cloud cover on the earth which absorbs energy in the atmosphere from the sun causing warming and cooling cycles. This mechanism, if proven definitively, has little do do with carbon emissions in our atmosphere, and is not man-made nor controllable by man.

The real problem is the science. What makes a greenhouse gas function in the role of warming the atmosphere is the ability to absorb infrared radiation, and this depends on the molecular vibrations of the molecule that allow the molecules to absorb and re-emit incident radiation. Carbon Dioxide (GO_2 weight 44), is heavier than nitrogen (NI weight 28) or oxygen (O weight 32) and those are the major gaseous components in the atmosphere, but the lighter gases, water (H_2O weight 18) or methane (CH_4 weight 16), also found in the atmosphere, are much stronger infrared absorbers by virtue of their OH and CH chemical bonds, respectively. Methane is increasing slowly but carbon dioxide is still in greater concentration in the atmosphere and is more under control of mankind than methane which results mainly from anaerobic decomposition of organic matter. Therefore, adaptability is where our focus should be, not on a 'cap and trade' tax increase policy during a deep recession in the U.S. and Europe.

The observed response of climate to more CO_2 is not in good agreement with predictions, according to physicist, William Happer, in an Op Ed article in The Wall Street Journal on March 27, 2012. In fact, based on NOAA data, nothing has happened in global temperatures over the past decade. The latest monthly (February, 2012) global temperature anomaly for the lower atmosphere was minus 0.12 degrees Celsius, slightly less than the average since the satellite record of temperatures began in 1979. Therefore, the lack of statistically significant temperature data of unusual warming over the last decade, leaves the causal effect of CO_2 to global warming suspect at best.

CO_2 is not the problem. In fact, life on earth flourished for hundreds of millions of years at much higher levels of CO_2 than today! Increasing CO_2

levels will be a net benefit to the planet because cultivated plants grow better and are more resistant to draught at higher CO_2 levels.

There are actually two competing theories to explain climate change. Therefore, the prudent strategy is improved energy efficiency technologies implementation, the best and sole path to reducing global warming, and thereby, averting climate change.

Anecdotes

1) unemployment insurance
2) social security benefits
3) productivity v. unemployment, I.e., the productivity trap (high productivity generates high unemployment), i.e., Labor Union Curve
4) Phillips Curve: inflation v. unemployment obsolete
4) Federal Reserve Bank & monetary policy
5) food stamps
6) welfare checks
7) philanthropy (philanthropic capitalism), e.g., the Global Fund, The Melissa & Bill Gates Foundation, the Rockefeller Foundation, etc.
8) charitable gifts deducted from income tax payments
9) innovation breeds unemployment, I.e., slippery slope to recessions or depressions
10) creative destruction theory of capitalism, I.e., continuously destroys itself then recreates itself (Marx) & (Schumpeter)

Author
Dr. Richard E. Itteilag
Jupiter,FL
June, 2012

References:

http://data.bls.gov/pdq/SurveyOutputServlet?request_action=wh&graph_name=LN_cpsbref3
http://data.bls.gov/pdq/SurveyOutputServlet?request_action=wh&graph_name=LN_cpsbref3